BIOLOGY Field Notes

Be a GIRAFFE Expert

by
E. C. Andrews

Minneapolis, Minnesota

Credits

All images are courtesy of Shutterstock.com, unless otherwise specified. With thanks to Getty Images, Thinkstock Photo, and iStockphoto.

Recurring – LadadikArt, Milano M, The_Pixel, yana shypova, vectorplus, Macrovector, NotionPic, Devita ayu silvianingtyas. Character throughout – NotionPic. Cover – jaroslava V, Devita ayu silvianingtyas, Christopher Robin Smith Photography, The_Pixel, Milano M, vectorplus, Macrovector. 4–5 – Volodymyr Burdiak, Christoph Hilger, EcoPic. 6–7 – Quinton Meyer ZA, etienneb07. 8–9 – Pelow Media, yod 67. 10–11 – Bryan Busovicki, tonyzhao120. 12–13 – Henk Bogaard, John Michael Vosloo. 14–15 – LizCoughlan, imageBROKER.com. 16–17 – meunierd, ChrisVanLennepPhoto. 18–19 – S.Jeshurun Vineeth Roshan, Balamurugan veerabathiran. 20–21 – Vladimir Turkenich, Craig Fraser. 22–23 – mobrafotografie, Martin Pelanek.

Bearport Publishing Company Product Development Team

Publisher: Jen Jenson; Director of Product Development: Spencer Brinker; Managing Editor: Allison Juda; Editor: Cole Nelson; Associate Editor: Naomi Reich; Associate Editor: Tiana Tran; Designer: Kim Jones; Designer: Kayla Eggert; Designer: Steve Scheluchin; Production Specialist: Owen Hamlin

Library of Congress Cataloging-in-Publication Data is available at www.loc.gov or upon request from the publisher.

ISBN: 979-8-89577-004-7 (hardcover)
ISBN: 979-8-89577-435-9 (paperback)
ISBN: 979-8-89577-121-1 (ebook)

© 2026 BookLife Publishing
This edition is published by arrangement with BookLife Publishing.

North American adaptations © 2026 Bearport Publishing Company. All rights reserved. No part of this publication may be reproduced in whole or in part, stored in any retrieval system, or transmitted in any form or by any means, electronic, mechanical, photocopying, recording, or otherwise, without written permission from the publisher. Bearport Publishing is a division of FlutterBee Education Group.

For more information, write to Bearport Publishing, 5357 Penn Avenue South, Minneapolis, MN 55419.

CONTENTS

Meet the Biologist............4

A Giraffe's Body 6

Grassy Homes 10

Towers 12

Dinner Time.................14

Tall Talkers 16

No Bedtime 18

Life Cycle...................20

Giant Giraffes...............22

Glossary....................24

Index 24

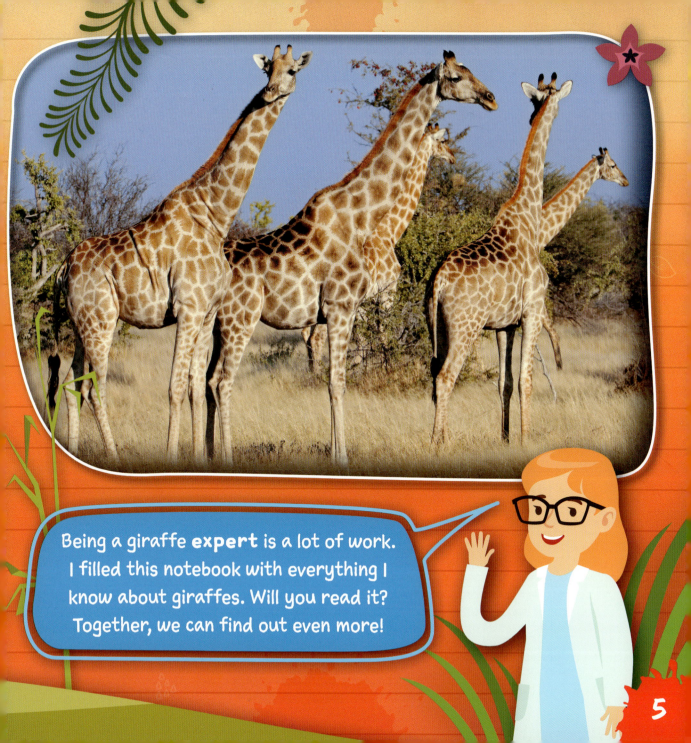

Being a giraffe **expert** is a lot of work. I filled this notebook with everything I know about giraffes. Will you read it? Together, we can find out even more!

A GIRAFFE'S BODY

Giraffes use their long necks to reach high trees for food. From above, they can also watch out for **predators**. Sometimes, giraffes get into fights with one another over who is in charge. Then, they use their necks to battle.

Giraffe necks are often 6 feet (2 m) long.

These tall mammals can be fast when they need to. Long legs help giraffes make a quick getaway if they spot a predator. When predators get too close, giraffes can deliver a nasty kick!

Giraffes can reach speeds up to 35 miles per hour (56 kph).

Strong tongues allow giraffes to eat spiky plants. Their tongues are also very long. This helps giraffes reach all their favorite foods.

Scientists believe giraffe tongues are a dark color to keep them from getting sunburned.

A giraffe's tongue

Every giraffe has a special pattern of spots. A mother can recognize her baby by its spots. The brown-colored spots also help giraffes **camouflage** themselves. This hides them from predators.

A baby giraffe is called a calf.

GRASSY HOMES

Giraffes in the wild are found in Africa. They live in habitats called savannas, which are a type of grassland. African savannas have a wet season and a dry season.

A habitat is the place where a plant or animal lives.

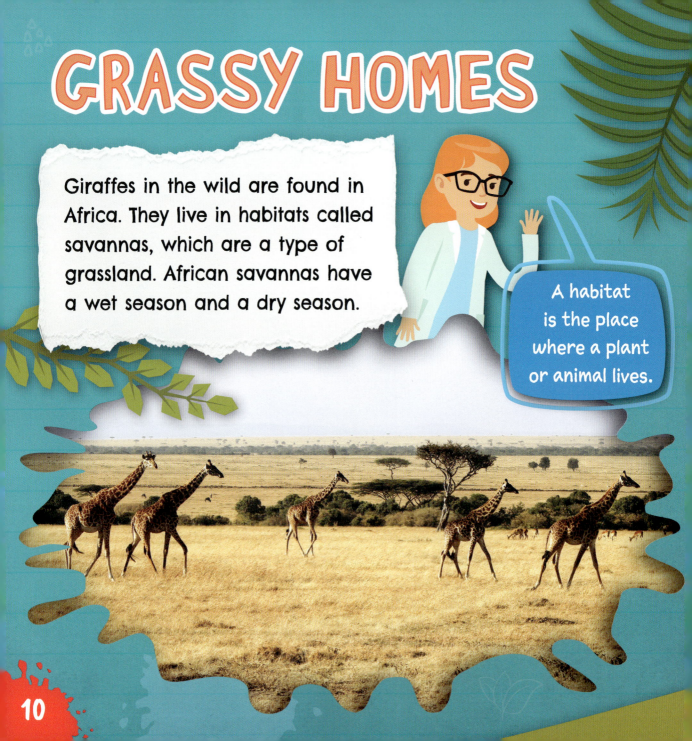

Giraffes get most of the water they need from the leaves they eat.

There is hardly any rain during the dry season. However, the wet season has lots of rain to help plants grow. This provides giraffes with food.

11

TOWERS

Groups of giraffes are called towers or herds. A tower usually has 10 to 20 giraffes in it. Being in a tower helps keep giraffes safe from predators.

There are four different **species** of giraffes. People used to think there was only one!

Giraffe babies have close **bonds** with their mothers. Nuzzling helps mother giraffes and their calves learn each other's scent. When the young giraffes grow up, they are free to leave or to stay with their tower.

Giraffe mothers in a tower take turns looking after all the calves while others search for food.

A mother giraffe

A calf

DINNER TIME

Giraffes are herbivores. That means they eat only plants. These tall mammals munch on a lot of twigs and leaves that other animals cannot reach. Their favorite leaves come from acacia trees.

An acacia tree

Giraffes can eat more than 100 pounds (45 kg) of food per day.

Giraffes have stomachs with four different parts. This helps them break down their food completely. Their stomachs let them eat small amounts of poisonous plants without getting sick. The poison kills **parasites** inside their bodies but does not hurt the giraffes.

TALL TALKERS

Many people might think giraffes do not make any noise. But that is because humans cannot hear the sounds giraffes make. These mammals often use low-pitched noises to **communicate** with one another.

The low sound that giraffes use can travel long distances. A lot of predators cannot hear it. This helps the animals communicate without predators knowing where they are.

Sometimes, giraffes make mooing sounds to communicate.

NO BEDTIME

Do giraffes need sleep? They do, but not very much. Giraffes can get through the day with hardly any sleep at all. In fact, they just need about 30 minutes of it!

Instead of sleeping for a long stretch of time, giraffes take quick naps throughout the day. They sleep for only about five minutes at a time. Giraffes can even snooze while standing up!

Shh! Don't wake up the giraffe.

LIFE CYCLE

How does the giraffe life cycle start? A mother giraffe carries a baby inside her for about 15 months. She usually gives birth to only one calf at a time. A baby giraffe can sometimes walk within one hour of being born!

A life cycle includes the different stages of an animal's life.

The **females** in a tower protect the calves from predators. Mother giraffes also teach their young what they can and cannot eat. By the time they are four to six years old, the calves have grown into adults. Many will later start families of their own.

Giraffes live for about 25 years.

GIANT GIRAFFES

From their long legs to their even longer necks, giraffes are giant creatures! I hope you've enjoyed learning about these amazing mammals.

GLOSSARY

biologist a person who studies and knows a lot about living things

bonds close connections or friendships

camouflage to hide by blending in with the surroundings

communicate to share information

expert a person who knows a lot about something

females giraffes that can give birth to babies

mammals animals that are warm-blooded, drink milk from their mothers when they are young, and have fur

parasites creatures that get food by living on or in another plant or animal

predators animals that hunt other animals for food

species groups that animals are divided into, according to similar characteristics

INDEX

calves 9, 13, 20–21
females 21
food 6, 8, 11, 13, 15
habitats 10
leaves 11, 14

legs 7, 22
necks 6, 22
predators 6–7, 9, 12, 17, 21
spots 9

towers 12–13, 21
trees 6, 14
twigs 14